WILD SWIMMING

AT SCARWEATHER SANDS

WILD SWIMMING AT SCARWEATHER SANDS

ROBERT MINHINNICK

THE BLACK SPRING
PRESS GROUP

First published in 2023
by Eyewear Publishing Ltd.,
an imprint of Black Spring Publishing Group
United Kingdom

Typeset with graphic design by Edwin Smet
Cover image by Eamon Bourke

ISBN 978-1-915406-39-2

BLACKSPRINGPRESSGROUP.COM

To wild swimmers and beachcombers everywhere.

TABLE OF CONTENTS

INTRODUCTION

Warfare, piracy, wrecking, the weather, and yes, swimming, dominate this writing.

All locations are explicit, centred on Scarweather Sands and Sker Point, close to the resort of Porthcawl in south Wales.

The Ordnance Survey references will allow walkers and swimmers to explore these places. But be warned, the terrain is difficult and the tide can be lethal. Remember, the Bristol Channel has the second highest tidal range in the world.

Yet exploring here is fascinating, especially as a warming climate and rising sea levels mean new discoveries for beachcombing. Because all readers have always been wild swimmers and beachcombers.

And of course, they have to learn to read the tides, both high and low. As these writings state, every twelve hours it all begins again.

1. CASTELL MORLAIS

Castell Morlais, Porthcawl has been described as 'Uncertain'[1] *but is rejected as such. There are no visible remains.*

OS Map Grid Reference[2]*: SS80297826*
Latitude 51.49042° Longitude -3.72602°

Fanciful? A folly? Or a map of the cartographer's imagination?

A cholera hospital for an earlier epidemic supported by Florence Nightingale? A lime pit for hanged smugglers and the wreckers who heard the Riot Act read on the sands?

I swim on and swim on even though I cannot swim.
It's all a dream I have when wild swimming, cave to cove through the limestone gutters and the drowned men's fingers or sea hemlock as some call seaweed here...

I've seen the megaliths at Carnac, *Les Geants de Kerzerho* and understand there are other stones beneath the tides and that the ocean will never confess its crimes...

So I swim on and swim on even though I cannot swim. Now I climb through the quartz rainbow at Ffynnon Wen and feel I understand this coast at last, each colour a quotation and a clue.

But with the next tide the air darkens and I must seek the castle whilst its fable grows stranger.
I might even learn the sonic alphabet of porpoises. But is there some inexplicable wisdom in their clicks and wheezes?

---

1 http://www.gatehouse-gazetteer.info/key.html
2 https://getoutside.ordnancesurvey.co.uk/guides/beginners-guide-to-grid-references/

So I swim on and swim on even though I cannot swim. And if I follow this coast it comes to me that such dreams are there only for those who dare the sea's delirium...

2. GWTER HOPSOG

Category: Geographic Feature
Type: Other Coastal Landform
Latitude/Longitude: 51°28'51"N, *3°43'15"W*
Eastings/Northings: 280599, 177190

We needed wood so I descended the moraine beside this inlet, its pebbles almost impossible...

But I knew, after a while, something had died here recently. And there it was beside my driftwood stack, a black-skulled porpoise, piebald, ripe and discarded by its element, eternal purpose served by this dark sea-deer, Atlantic acrobat, a last harbour here at Hopsog, wood and weed its pyre which I've seen burn green as iodine...

Then twelve hours later it all begins again.

3. GWTER GRYN-Y-LOCS

Other Coastal Landform
Latitude/Longitude: 51°29'2"N, *3°43'23"W*
Eastings/Northings: 280444, 177537
OS Grid: SS804775

After all this time most of my limestone
vocabulary is returning as up I go, recalling
every crease and crevice in the rock, the wrinkles
a fingernail might fit, then over the shoulder, stark edifice,
to stand at a pool's rim looking down and balancing
on a razorblade.

*

Even with eyes closed I could see the lightning, an X-ray
of the cliff after that bonecrack thunder. Even with eyes closed
I could see everything, though I had left my glasses
in the grass all night, the lenses two dewed moons,
a pair of clouds.

And I realise I might never see again the constellation I had craned
towards, rubbing my eyes as if that would lift the frost from my sight...

*

Teardrops, these lead sinkers on the Gwter wall. In rock pools, the
nylon lines go on forever, and the hooks take deadly directions to
another glazed eye,
a twisted mouth.

This is why next time I will carry a knife. Carry a knife...

*

Yet I might wait a lifetime here... Perhaps I already have...

With me are two collared doves, each with its black gorget, a nervous pair, bonfire smoke their smudges on the air.

Fools, I call them, these lovebirds, drab as seafoam in this Gwter Gryn but faithful in their grey monogamy.

*

Marram the waves, serrated this sea, salving its wounds with its saltings but thank god
for the straw hat.

Time after time we fill it with sand to pour over the charcoal, still white.

Once, a child fell into such coals to leap from her own skin, that silver bag out of which she stepped newborn across the beach...

*

This water's sure to be cold but in I step, whitefooted, the sand already swallowing me.

There are whirlpools while the moon tonight will float within this crevasse. Rise, wanton rise.

Yes, every atom, that's what was clear in the thunderflash. And I ask, why didn't it drive me mad, the dust, the dirt, the meteors of my mind?

Because what I saw you'd never believe. You wouldn't dare.

But it was there! The august triangle with Vega, fat and blue and all the fairground stars rushing away from me. What could I do but embrace that ascension?

Then twelve hours later it all begins again.

4. SCARWEATHER

Bank
Location: United Kingdom, Britain and Ireland, Europe
Latitude: 51.4833° or 51° 29' north
Longitude: -3.85° or 3° 51' west

Ar fôr tymhestlog teithio 'rwyf'

Apricocks? I tasted one. Yellow apples but with black stones. Three hundred aboard, the captain claimed, but the sea was crashing through the canyons, its cannonballs rolling round the deck.

I cried out in every language I knew but who was listening? Three hundred souls lost at Scarweather Sands, land where no land should be. Because not every place is written on the charts. And some are written where no place ever was...

I could have told them all they needed to know but we were blown into the channels at Gwter y Cwn, deck to bilge the ship riven – African slaves or press-ganged sailors – the waves did not discriminate and I felt the ocean boil beneath my feet, potholes and blowholes and waterspouts.

Three hundred aboard, the captain claimed but once you're in that terrible maze you can never get out... The Receiver of Wreck to be notified, the lading bills lost, the brandy casks and the silk in its bolts shredded on the rocks...

I awoke at dawn in the pit of Pwll Dafan, sun splinters in my eyes, bloody salt stiff on my sleeves... and such a thirst on me as I've never known.

Determined, that sea... seeking me through the storm... They said we were at war but I've never even seen a Frenchie.

Three hundred aboard, the captain claimed,
and all but me drownded.

5. FFYNNON WEN

Name: Ffynnon-wen Rocks, Bridgend (Pen-y-bont)
Place type: Other Coastal Landform
Location: Grid Ref: SS 7985 7877 • X/Y co-ords: 279858, 178770
Lat/Long: 51.49509811, -3.73205478

A life, of sorts, undoubtedly a life. I live it at the waves' edge in the white quartz...

That life spent listening to shells... But how else should I spend my time?

Salt around the pools today like chalk where the dead bodies lay. Yet somehow a promise will be kept.

Towers of smoke above this beach, its clints and grykes all rains might reach. But wait...
Were there volcanoes on Gower?

*

I've been to Pompeii and seen the last bus arrive, its timetable scorched under an inch of ash, the slaves buried alive, the prostitutes buried alive, the gladiators buried alive, the dogwalkers carrying plastic bags buried alive, the sunbathers smeared in factor 40 buried alive, the lifeguards with their highlights and Samoan tattoos buried alive, the brawling boys and their silver whippets buried alive, the philosophers in their caves buried alive, the girl who sells Mivvis and Magnums and Soleros buried alive.

And not all of them two metres apart. Thank the gods I always wear a mask.

*

So who are the people who build these driftwood shacks and lie with the bonewhite dead we all must become? Are our children the fossils of the future?

Might be millennia ago or a part of next year's fairground pixels.

Yet a life, of sorts, undoubtedly a life lived at the waves' edge in the white quartz...

A hut for one night... built from driftwood and the sea's plastic. Yes, something once flourished here. And might so again?

The cults will rise and rule and fall away. Eons it might take but eventually each tribe returns to its territory.

Sandstone like blood under the sea and veins of quartz that have lead me here, but who are these people building with sticks white as ivory?

*

A life of sorts, undoubtedly a life, lived at the waves' edge in the white quartz...
Now and then and now and then golf balls and jellyfish at Ffynnon Wen, towers of smoke above the steelworks beach or the scalding rain and burning light of the Vesuvian night...

Salt around the pools today like chalk where once the bodies
lay and no way back until this driftwood reassembles itself – its
sticks white as ivory – and we can all lay ourselves down amongst
its terrible
bones...

6. PWLL DAFAN

Place type: Tidal Water
Location: Grid Ref: SS 7868 7959 • X/Y co-ords: 278688, 179594
Lat/Long: 51.50220108, -3.74919634
Height: -3.1m

So I swim on and swim on even though I cannot swim. I swim into this pool and reach the surface. Looking round now, the water bright, masks of all colours in its crevices.

And I recall how once I floated in the Dead Sea. Opening my eyes the sun upon me was a furnace mouth, in the hills above the hidden scrolls awaiting discovery...

I hauled myself out wearing my suit of salt. But here I swim on and swim on, thinking of all the lost books, of the mummies returned to life, and how our best work is never written down...

Then twelve hours later it all begins again...

7. GWTER Y CWN

Name: Gwter y Cwn (wetland / tidal), Bridgend (Pen-y-bont ar Ogwr)
Place type: Wetland
Location: Grid Ref: SS 7895 7941 • X/Y co-ords: 278957, 179412
Lat/Long: 51.50070190, -3.74525391

Last night a continent was drowned here.
Today I watch it emerge steaming.
A porpoise's black pup...

Nowhere as dangerous as this: its channels
and falls and fissures.

A corpse wrapped in a sail, a captain lashed to a mast...

Then twelve hours later it all begins again...

8. BWT HAFN

Place type: Other Coastal Landform
Location: Grid Ref: SS 7863 7968 • X/Y co-ords: 278639, 179683
Lat/Long: 51.50299835, -3.74992257
County/Unitary Authority: Bridgend (Pen-y-bont ar Ogwr)
Height: -3.1m

I confess not opening my eyes underwater. But so much we see is wishful thinking...

Once, I swear, I saw my daughter afloat in a lagoon at Sker. But there are generations of the drowned with me now...

Here is the steel beach, sinter-spread, wrecks unrecognizable, cannons washed overboard.

And when I stand the water is silver as the goosegrass of my childhood. *Priest's lice* it was called once. Still clinging to some yet so many brush it away...

I was press ganged out of one language and cast away in an alien anchorage.

Are those footprints showing the way to travel?
In the same moment, the brontosaurus, the dancing girl and medusa are moving towards and away from me.
So I swim on.

I swim on and swim on even though I cannot swim...

9. TUSKER ROCK / YNYS DYSGYR

As seen from the Wales Coastal Path

Category: Island
Location: Wales, United Kingdom, Britain and Ireland, Europe
Latitude: 51.4542° or 51° 27' 15.2" north
Longitude: -3.6697° or 3° 40' 11.1" west
Open Street Map ID: node 2388658478

Then turning east into history I discover
here's a saltwater litany we all speak
but it will never be complete...

Below me, Tysgyr starts with a shadow
then grows to five different scars
– an archipelago of sorts –

but soon the atoll itself is revealed,
its iron glints and ship's copper boiler
part of the limestone now...

I think of the Amazon
the George
the Mary
the Malleny
the Henry
the Dasher
the Nuestra Señora del Carmen.

The smacks, the brigs and barques, the sloops of war
and often the Vainqueur at Sker and Scarweather Sands.
This vessel in the wrong ocean.

Le Havre lost in the hurricane,
then simply
not there at all.

In her hold she was carrying
        789 chests of oranges
          650 frails of figs
            240 boxes of lemons
              84 planks of Brazilian hardwood.

Unknown is the number of locals
who drank themselves to death
with the ship's brandy…

The looters stripped the captain's body
of seventeen Portuguese gold reals,

  his silver shoes,
    his silver watch,
      his knee buckles.

There's a saltwater litany
we all speak
but it will never be complete…

The Brothers   The Richard   The George
The Liban, the James Grey
the Nuestra Señora del Carmen

The smacks, the brigs and barques, the sloops of war
and often the Vainqueur at Sker and Scarweather Sands.
This vessel in the wrong ocean.

Le Havre lost in the hurricane,
then simply
not there at all.

NOTES

'Castell Morlais' means Morlais Castle. Despite having an Ordnance reference, no trace of any structure can be found in this location. It is possible that a cholera hospital, Florence Nightingale, smugglers, wreckers and lime pits were all, at different times, associated with this place.

Ar fôr tymhestlog teithio 'rwyf' ('Scarweather'), this is from a Welsh language hymn, by Ieuan Glan Geirionydd, 'On a tempestuous sea I journey'.

'brontosaurus', 'dancing girl' and 'medusa' ('Bwt Hafn') are either prehistoric or Roman relics from Porthcawl.

'Silver whippets' ('Ffynnon Wen'), this is one of many English slang names for nitrous oxide canisters.

Welsh language place names depend on the Welsh alphabet, not the English. Discovering what they mean is as exciting as beachcombing. Go on, explore the Welsh language!

ACKNOWLEDGEMENTS

I'd like to thank the editors of poetry magazines and anthologies where some of these poems have appeared previously:

New Welsh Review; *Gorwelion/Shared Horizons*; *Archipelago*; *Long Poem Magazine*.